D0177582

Cumbria
County Council

Once there was a Seed

For Nellie - J.A

For Caiden, Lucy and Ben - M.G

First published in 2009 by Wayland

Wayland, 338 Euston Road, London NW1 3BH

Wayland Australia
Level 17/207 Kent Street
Sydney NSW 2000

Editor: Nicola Edwards
Designer: Paul Cherrill
Digital Colour: Carl Gordon

British Library Cataloguing in Publication Data

Anderson, Judith, 1965-
Once there was a seed
1. Seeds - Juvenile literature 2. Plant life cycles - Juvenile literature
I. Title II. Gordon, Mike
581.4'67

ISBN: 978 0 7502 5644 5

Printed in China

Wayland is a division of Hachette Children's Books, an Hachette UK company. www.hachettelivre.co.uk

Nature's Miracles

Once there was a Seed

Written by
Judith Anderson

Illustrated by
Mike Gordon

WAYLAND

Grandad loves
growing things.

He says he has green fingers. He says I have green fingers, too.

"Green fingers" means being good at growing things.

Today we're going to
plant some seeds.

First we push the seeds into some soil.

Grandad says that seeds
need three things to grow.

They need water,
warmth and light.

When a seed has water and warmth, a little root starts to grow out of it.

The root grows downwards.

Next, a little shoot grows out of the seed. The shoot grows upwards.

When it reaches the light,
it starts to sprout leaves.

Grandad says plants are just
like us. They need food to grow.
We get our food at mealtimes.
Plants make their own food
from water, light and air.

Below the soil, the roots are getting bigger and spreading further.

Above the soil, the plant is growing taller.

When the plant is big enough,
some new buds appear.

These buds turn into flowers.

Flowers come in many colours
and shapes. Some smell sweet,
too. Grandad says they look and
smell good so that he can win
a prize at the flower show.

But I think it is so that insects will notice them.

Flowers contain pollen.
When an insect visits
a flower, pollen sticks
to its body.

When the insect flies to another flower, the pollen goes, too.

One flower swaps pollen with another flower. Then the flower dies, but it leaves behind new seeds.

Conkers are seeds, too.
Ouch!

Before seeds grow into new plants, they need to find their own patch of soil. Often they are carried by the wind.

Sometimes a bird
helps them.

Sometimes
a squirrel
helps them.

And sometimes
Grandad helps them.

NOTES FOR PARENTS AND TEACHERS

Suggestions for reading the book with children

As you read this book with children, you may find it helpful to stop and discuss what is happening page by page. Children might like to talk about what the pictures show, and point out the changes taking place in the plants and trees. What other types of leaves, flowers, fruits and seeds are they familiar with?

The idea of a life cycle is developed throughout the book, and reinforced on the final pages when it becomes clear that the plant that was once a seed has now produced seeds of its own. Ask the children if they know of any other life cycles. Can they see any patterns in nature? The other titles in the series may help them think about this.

Discussing the subject of seeds and plants may introduce children to a number of unfamiliar words, including root, shoot, bud and pollen. Make a list of new words and discuss what they mean.

Nature's Miracles and the National Curriculum

The **Nature's Miracles** series satisfies a number of requirements of the Science curriculum at Key Stage 1. There are four titles about cycles in nature in the series: *Nature's Miracles: Once There Was a Seed; Once There Was a Caterpillar; Once There Was a Tadpole* and *Once There Was a Raindrop*. Each book encourages children to explore the natural world for themselves through direct observation and specific activities and emphasises developing a sense of responsibility towards plants, animals and natural resources.

Once There Was a Seed will help young readers to think about conditions for growth and stages of growth encountered in the units on 'Growing plants' and 'Helping plants to grow well', as well as providing learning and discussion opportunities for the units on 'Habitats', 'Variation' and 'Life cycles'.

Suggestions for follow-up activities

The little girl in this book plants a seed and watches it grow. Planting seeds and caring for young plants is a fun and rewarding activity, whether or not you have access to a garden. All you need are some seeds, a container and a growing medium – it doesn't even have to be soil. A carrot top in a saucer of water or cress seeds sprinkled on a damp tissue all help to demonstrate the need for light, warmth and water.

Choosing which seeds or plants to grow is great fun, and encourages children to think about variety and habitat. Do you have enough space for sunflowers? Bulbs such as daffodils might make an interesting alternative. Would vegetables or fruit be a good idea? Seed potatoes will grow in a pot if it is large enough, as will tomatoes.

Once the seeds or bulbs have been planted, explain that it may take some time before a shoot appears. Encourage children to think about warmth, light and water. How much does the plant need? Can it have too much? Is there anything else that might harm the plant's chances?

Books to read

Ten Seeds by Ruth Brown (Andersen Press, 2001)
Learning about Life Cycles: The life cycle of a Rose by Ruth Thomson (Wayland, 2008)
Life Cycles: Sunflower by Ruth Thomson (*Popcorn* series) (Wayland, 2009)

Useful websites

www.bigeyedowl.co.uk/activities-growing.htm.
www.bbc.co.uk/gardening/gardening_with_children/plantstotry_index.shtml

Index